Learn HTML, CSS, and JavaScript With This One Book

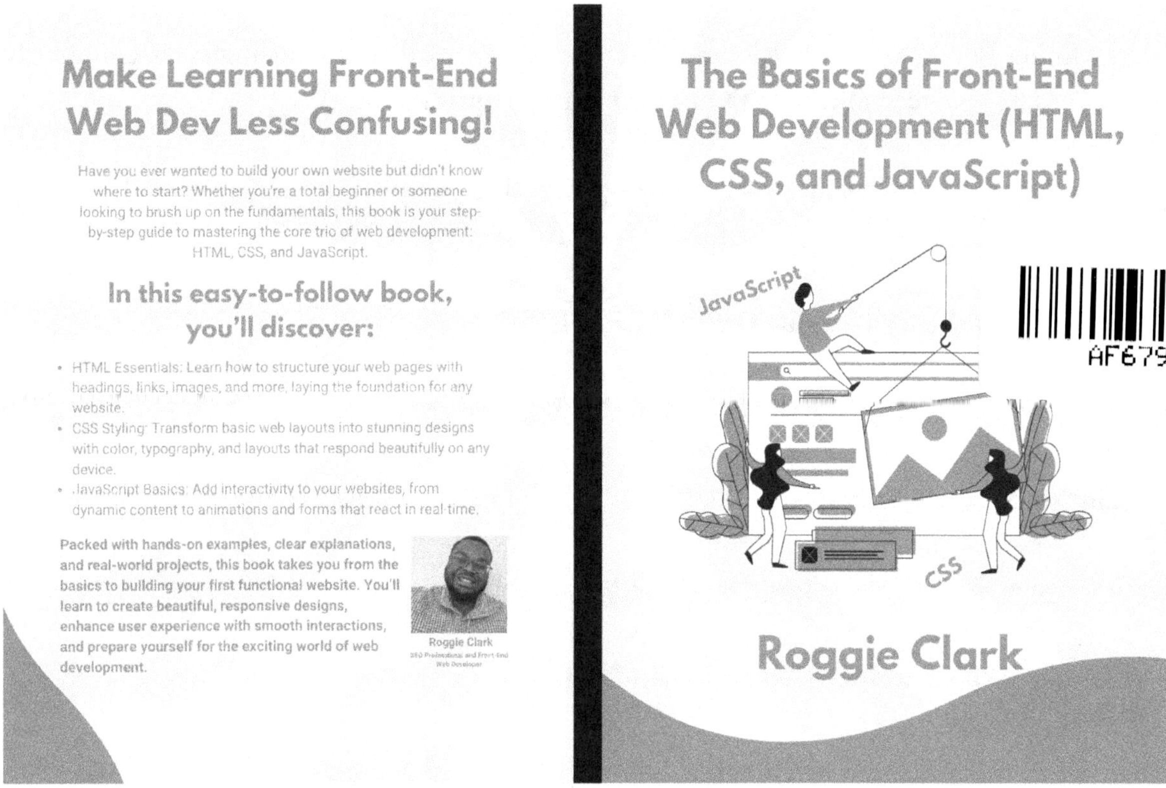

Please note; that this book is just the HTML chapter of the full book; the **Basics of Front-End Web Development (HTML, CSS, and JavasScript)**. To learn all three coding languages, check out the full book.

https://www.amazon.com/Basics-Front-End-Development-HTML-JavaScript-ebook/dp/B0DJ147B15

Learn SEO Too

Learning front-end web development is only half the battle to producing an amazing web experience. Also, you need to learn **SEO (search engine optimization)**.

Learning SEO ensures that visitors can <u>actually</u> find your website and apps on the internet. Below I included links to several SEO books I've written. They are excellent reads.

The ABCs of SEO: Search Engine Optimization 101

https://www.amazon.com/ABCs-Search-Engine-Optimization-Page-ebook/dp/B0C2JSLW7M

The Technical SEO Handbook

https://www.amazon.com/Technical-SEO-Handbook-Learn-Issues-ebook/dp/B0CMBJR9QV

The SEO and Web Developer Collaboration Guide

https://www.amazon.com/SEO-Web-Developer-Collaboration-Guide-ebook/dp/B0DHLBM48C

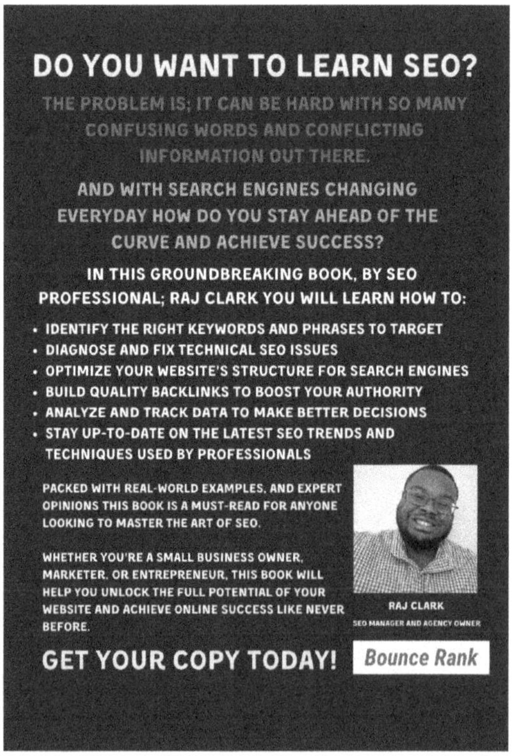

The HTML (Hypertext Markup Language) Coding For Beginners

By: Roggie Clark

Copyright

Title: The Basics of HTML (Hypertext Markup Language) Coding For Beginners
Author: Roggie Clark

Cover Design: Roggie Clark
Editing: Renee' Clark

Printed in the United States of America

Disclaimer

The views and opinions expressed in this book are those of the author and do not necessarily reflect the official policy or position of any individual, company, or organization cited or referenced in the text.

The author is not affiliated with any of the individuals, companies, or organizations mentioned in the text, nor does the author receive any form of compensation for citing or referencing them. Some sample scenarios in this text are fictitious. Any similarity to actual persons, living or dead, is coincidental.

The professional information (strategies, tips, and concepts) in this text is distributed on an "as is" basis, without warranty. While every precaution has been taken in the preparation of the text to ensure all information is accurate, neither the author nor the publisher shall have any liability to any person or entity with respect to any loss or damage caused or alleged to be caused directly or indirectly by the instructions contained in this text or by the computer software and hardware products described in it.

Neither the author nor the publisher guarantees any specific results or outcomes, and the information provided in this text should not be construed as professional advice. Readers should always consult with a qualified professional before making any significant changes to their website or business.

By reading this text, you agree that the author nor the publisher is responsible for any direct, indirect, incidental, or consequential damages that may arise from the use of the information provided. You assume full responsibility for any actions taken based on the information presented in this text.

Table of Contents

Chapter 1: Introduction

Welcome to the beginning of your journey into the wonderful world of website development! Imagine this: you're standing at the gateway of the internet, and in your hand is a key—**HTML**, or **Hypertext Markup Language**.

This key doesn't just open doors; it lets you build them. With HTML, you're no longer just browsing the web—you're creating it. You're setting the stage for all the beautiful, interactive, and exciting websites and web apps that billions of people will use. Whether you're building a personal blog, a portfolio to showcase your talents or the next big app, HTML is where it all starts.

Once you master the basics of HTML, you'll be able to:

- Craft stunning webpages from scratch that look just the way you imagined them.

- Share your thoughts, art, or business with the world in ways that reflect your unique style.

- Collaborate with others in the digital space, creating content that reaches the globe.

- Open the door to more advanced skills like CSS, JavaScript, and beyond!

The best part? You don't need to be a genius or a techie to learn this stuff. HTML is a beginner-friendly coding language, that anyone can pick up quickly. Before you know it you will be coding like a pro!

So, buckle up, because, by the end of this book, you'll have the foundation to not just navigate the web, but to build your own corner of it. So with that being said, let's get into chapter 1, the basics, and that is what HTML is in simple words.

Chapter 2: What is HTML

HyperText Markup Language (HTML) is the *standard markup* or computer code that is used to create and structure content on the web. Web browsers can "render" (display) HTML on a user's computer screen, in a format readable for the user. (Wikipedia, n.d.).

Created by Sir Timothy John Berners-Lee; HTML was designed, in 1989, as an easy-to-use and effective method for creating documents for the World Wide Web.

At the time the internet was still in its infancy stage, and there wasn't a clear way to create and structure content on web pages.

Users often would send *FTP (File Transfer Protocol)* files to each other to display their work online, but these files were often bulky, fragmented, and not searchable or accessible to other users.

HTML was able to address this issue by allowing developers to embed their content in the form of clickable text, or *hypertext,* which users can create using *elements* also sometimes referred to as *tags*.

Tags are specific pieces of code meant to represent the parts of the document. The tags are similar to the common features of a book, like titles, headers, paragraphs, lists, etc.

To make things even more accessible, users are also able to "link" or connect documents using *hyperlinks.* Over time HTML has evolved to include other elements but the same basic functionality remains today (Wikipedia, n.d.).

Here's an example of a basic HTML document (W3School, n.d.):

```
<!DOCTYPE html>
<html>
     <head>
           </head>
          <body>

          </body>
</html>
```

Key Components of An HTML Document

Let's break down this example into its components, as you can see, HTML documents include several key elements such as: `<!DOCTYPE html>`. This is the statement that declares that the document is an HTML document. All HTML documents must include this statement.

Additionally, The `<!DOCTYPE html>` declaration is used to inform the browser which version of HTML the page is written in. In modern web development, we use **HTML5**, and `<!DOCTYPE html>`is the declaration for HTML5.

Next is the `<html>` element, which defines the start of the HTML document, it "wraps" around everything that's displayed on a webpage. It marks the beginning and end of the document.

Next is the `<head>` element. This tag represents the top or beginning of the HTML document. Additionally, it may contain meta-information about the page. This can include the title, meta tags (used for search engine optimization), and links to external resources such as JavaScript and/or CSS files. It does not contain content that will be visible to users.

Lastly, the `<body>` section contains the actual content that will be displayed on the webpage. It includes text, images, links, buttons, and anything else users will interact with.

There are additional, HTML tags that you will commonly see but before doing that I believe that it is important to establish a baseline understanding of HTML syntax first.

Chapter 3: How to Write HTML Properly

When writing HTML it is important to know the proper way to do it, this ensures that your code is easy to read and follow. Here's what you should know about HTML syntax:

1. Closing Tags and Self-Closing Elements:

- Most elements have **opening** (`<head>`) and **closing** tags (`</head>`). The content goes between these tags. As you can see, the `/` is used to represent the closing tag.
- Some tags, like `<img>` or `<br>`, are **self-closing** and don't need a closing tag. (We explore what these tags represent in the *common HTML Tags* section)
- Always make sure to close your tags (for elements that require a closing tag) and use self-closing syntax for elements like `<img>` and `<br>`.

---

2. Not Case-Sensitive:

- HTML tags are **not case-sensitive**, but the convention is to write them in **lowercase** (e.g., `<body>`, not `<Body>` or `<BODY>`). This improves readability and consistency.

---

3. HTML Attributes:

- Attributes provide additional information about an element. They are always written in the **opening tag** and come in name/value pairs, like href="https://example.com" in an *anchor tag* (<a>). We will explore *anchor tags* in greater detail in the *common HTML Tags* section
- The attribute value should be enclosed in **double quotes** (" "), though single quotes (' ') are technically allowed.

Example:

<a href="https://example.com" target="_blank">Visit Example</a>

---

4. Nesting and Proper Tag Hierarchy:

- HTML elements can be **nested** inside one another. However, proper **tag hierarchy** is crucial.
- Always close tags in the **reverse order** in which they were opened.

As you can recall from the previous code snippet I showed above:

```
<!DOCTYPE html>
<html>
     <head>
           </head>
          <body>

          </body>
</html>
```

Inside of the `<!DOCTYPE html>` element, the `<html>` is nested inside of it, and then nested inside of it, is the `<head>` element, and nested inside the `<html>` element is the `<body>` element.

Here is an example of incorrect nesting:

```
<!DOCTYPE html>
<html>
     <head><body></body></head>
</html>
```

As you can see the `<body>` element is incorrectly nested in the `<head>` element.

---

5. Indentation and Readability:

- Use consistent **indentation** to organize nested elements. This improves the readability of the code, especially for larger documents.
- Typically, a **two or four-space** indentation is used for each level of nesting.

Again recalling the code snippet example from above, notice how each tag starts on a new "line" again this improves readability.

```
<!DOCTYPE html>
<html>
     <head>
           </head>
          <body>

          </body>
</html>
```

---

6. HTML Comments:

- Comments are helpful for leaving notes in the code for future reference. They do not affect how the webpage is displayed.
- Comments are added using the syntax: <!-- Comment -->.

Example:

<!-- This is a comment explaining the code -->

<head></head>

Now that we discussed how to write HTML properly, let’s explore what are some common HTML elements that all novice front-end web developers should know.

Chapter 4: Important HTML Tags to Know

For novice front-end web developers, mastering common HTML tags is crucial to creating well-structured web pages. Here's a list of fundamental HTML tags every beginner should know:

1. Basic Structure Tags:

- <html>: The root element of an HTML document.
- <head>: Contains meta-information like title, styles, and scripts.
- <body>: Contains the content of the webpage (text, images, links, etc.).

---

2. Text and Content Tags:

- <h1> to <h6>: Header tags, with <h1> being the largest and usually the most important. Next is <h2> then <h3> next <h4>, <h5> and ending with <h6> as the smallest.
- <p>: Paragraph tag for blocks of text.
-
: Line break, creates a new line within text.
- <hr>: Horizontal rule, creates a horizontal line break.
- <strong>: Boldens text for emphasis (also conveys semantic meaning for search engine optimization).
- <em>: Italicizes text for emphasis (also conveys semantic meaning).

---

3. List Tags:

- <ul>: Unordered list (bulleted).
- <ol>: Ordered list (numbered).
- <li>: List item within <ul> or <ol>.

Additional Information On HTML List

To code an HTML list, you use different tags for ordered and unordered lists.

Unordered List (bulleted):

- Use the <ul> tag.

- Add list items inside it with the <li> tag.

Ordered List (numbered):

- Use the <ol> tag.

- Add list items inside it with the <li> tag.

Example:

Unordered List:

```
<ul>
  <li>Item 1</li>
  <li>Item 2</li>
  <li>Item 3</li>
</ul>
```

How it looks in HTML:

- Item 1
- Item 2
- Item 3

Ordered List:

```
<ol>
  <li>Item 1</li>
  <li>Item 2</li>
  <li>Item 3</li>
</ol>
```

How it looks in HTML:

1. Item 1
2. Item 2
3. Item 3

---

4. Link and Navigation Tags:

- <a>: Anchor tag for hyperlinks. Links to other pages or sections using the href attribute.
- <nav>: Defines a section for navigation links.

---

5. Media Tags:

- <img>: Embeds images using the src attribute to specify the image source.
- <video>: Embeds video content.
- <audio>: Embeds audio content.

---

6. Table Tags:

- <table>: Defines a table.
- <tr>: Table row.
- <td>: Table data (cell).
- <th>: Table header.

Additional Information On HTML Tables

HTML tables are a bit tricky to create so here's a bit of information on this. To code an HTML table, you use the <table> element and its child elements. Here's a quick guide:

1. Create the table using the <table> tag.

2. Define rows with <tr> (table row).

3. Add table headers using <th> (table header).

4. Add table data using <td> (table data cell).

Example:

```html
<table>
 <tr>
  <th>Header 1</th>
  <th>Header 2</th>
  <th>Header 3</th>
 </tr>
 <tr>
  <td>Data 1</td>
  <td>Data 2</td>
  <td>Data 3</td>
 </tr>
 <tr>
  <td>Data 4</td>
  <td>Data 5</td>
  <td>Data 6</td>
 </tr>
</table>
```

This will create a basic table with a header row and two rows of data. An example of how the HTML will be displayed is below.

Header 1	Header 2	Header 3
Data 1	Data 2	Data 3
Data 4	Data 5	Data 6

---

7. Form Tags:

- <form>: Creates an HTML form for user input.
- <input>: Defines an input field (e.g., text, checkbox, radio, etc.).
- <button>: Button for submitting forms or performing actions.
- <label>: Label for form elements.
- <textarea>: Multi-line text input field.

---

8. Grouping Tags:

- <div>: Division or container for structuring content.it is also called a *block-level element* because it is displayed on one line, and pushes non-block elements below or to the side of the block element.
- <span>: Inline container for styling or grouping small sections of text.
- <id>: this attribute is used to point to a specific style declaration in a style sheet (we will explore *stylesheets* in the *How CSS is added to HTML section* of the *CSS chapter*). It is also used by JavaScript (we will explore this in the *function section* of the *Javascript chapter*) to access and manipulate the element with the specific id.

---

10. Metadata Tags:

- <meta>: Provides metadata like character encoding, viewport settings, SEO tags. This tag is self closing.
- <link>: Links to external resources like stylesheets.

These tags form the foundation of HTML and are essential for structuring and presenting content on the web. Additionally, avoid deprecated elements. Some older HTML elements (like <font>or <center>) are **deprecated** in modern HTML5 and should not be used. Use **CSS** for styling and layout instead.

Now that we discuss common HTML tags to know, I believe it is important to discuss Semantic HTML and it's role in modern day HTML writing.

Chapter 5: Semantic HTML Explained

Additionally, it is worth noting that since the introduction of HTML5, several other elements have been added. When structuring webpages you should:

Use **semantic elements** (like `<article>`, `<section>`, etc.) to describe the content's structure and purpose. Instead of (`<div>` and `<span>` which don't tell anything about the content on the page.)

Additionally, Semantic HTML helps enhance the document's readability, accessibility, and SEO-friendliness.

Example:

```
<article>
  <header>
    <h1>Understanding Semantic HTML</h1>
  </header>
  <p>This article explains the importance of semantic HTML.</p>
</article>
```

Additional Semantic Tags (HTML5):

- **<header>**: Defines the header section of a webpage or section.
- <footer>: Defines the footer section.
- <section>: Groups-related content.
- <article>: Represents an independent piece of content.
- <aside>: Sidebar content related to the main content.
- <main>: The main content area of the document.

Below I included a graphic from W3Schools that I thought would also be helpful with giving you a general idea of hwo the tags should be layed out:

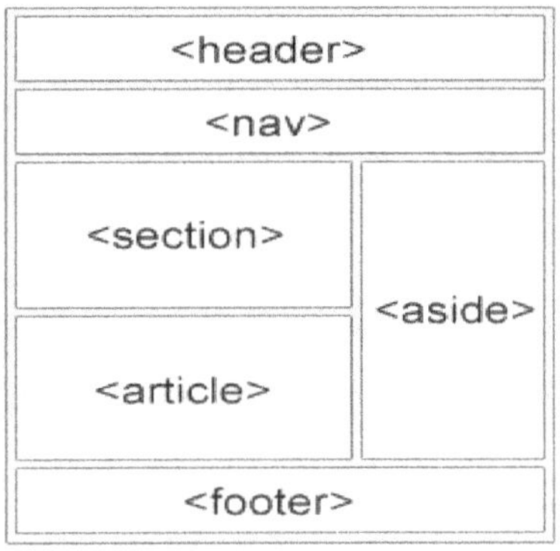

Cite From:https://www.w3schools.com/html/html5_semantic_elements.asp

Chapter 6: HTML and SEO

If you are familiar with SEO (search engine optimization), which if you are serious about creating websites, you should learn, there are additional tags/code snippets needed for optimal search engine performance, here they are:

- `<title>`This snippet is used to write a **Title tag** for the page, sometimes referred to as *Meta titles* or *Title links,* this tag is used by searchers to see what the name of the webpage is, and for some insight into what it is about, thus enticing them to click on the webpage.

- `<meta name="description" content="">`This snippet is used to write a **Meta Description** for the page. Similar to the Title Tag, the Meta description is to entice a reader to click on the webpage. Additionally, search engines use the meta description to explain to searchers what a webpage is about.

- `<meta name="robots" content="index, follow" >` This tag controls how search engines index and follow your page. A common value is index, follow, which allows search engines to index the page and follow its links.

- `<meta charset="UTF-8">` This code snippet indicates the *character encoding* or the types of symbols, and text used in the document. This matters because different languages have different symbols and characters, so using *UTF-8,* which is the standard that most search engines prefer, covers all of the possible characters used in any language.

- `<meta http-equiv="X-UA-Compatible" content="IE=edge">` This code snippet ensures that all Web browsers can properly display the document.

- `<meta name="viewport" content="width=device-width, initial-scale=1.0">` This code snippet ensures that the document is viewable on all devices, especially mobile devices.

Chapter 7: HTML Attributes

In HTML, attributes provide additional information about elements. They are always written inside the opening tag and are made up of a **name** and a **value**. The **name** specifies what kind of information is being given, and the **value** provides the information itself. For example:

```
<a href="https://example.com">Visit Example</a>
```

In the above example, `href` is the attribute name, and `"https://example.com"` is the value. Attributes enhance elements by providing extra data or modifying behavior.

Structure of HTML Attributes

1. **Name**: The attribute name (e.g., `href`, `id`, `class`).
2. **Value**: The value for that attribute is provided in quotes (e.g., `"https://example.com"`, `"header"`).

Attributes usually appear as **name-value pairs**, but some attributes are **boolean attributes** (such as `disabled`, `checked`, or `readonly`), which don't need a value but indicate the presence of a certain feature.

Common HTML Attributes

Here are the most commonly used HTML attributes that beginners should understand:

- `id`
  Defines a unique identifier for an element. Useful for targeting specific elements with CSS or JavaScript.

  ```
  <div id="header">This is the header</div>
  ```

- `class`
  Used to apply CSS styles or target multiple elements in JavaScript.

  ```
  <p class="intro">This is an introduction.</p>
  ```

- `style`
  Used to apply inline CSS styles directly to an element.

```
<h1 style="color: red;">Red Heading</h1>
```

- `href`
  Specifies the URL for a link.

```
<a href="https://example.com">Click Here</a>
```

- `src`
  Defines the source of an image, video, or script.

```
<img src="image.jpg" alt="Sample Image">
```

- `alt`
  Provides alternative text for images. Important for accessibility and SEO.

```
<img src="logo.png" alt="Company Logo">
```

- `title`
  Adds extra information, often displayed as a tooltip when the user hovers over the element.

```
<p title="This is a paragraph.">Hover over this text.</p>
```

- `target`
  Specifies where to open a linked document. Common values include:
  - `_blank` (open in a new tab or window)

- `_self` (default, opens in the same tab)

```
<a href="https://example.com" target="_blank">Open in New Tab</a>
```

- `rel`
  Defines the relationship between the current document and the linked document. Often used with `href`.

```
<a href="https://example.com" rel="noopener">External Link</a>
```

- `type`
  Specifies the type of an input field or script.

```
<input type="text" placeholder="Enter your name">
```

- `value`
  Defines the initial value for input elements like forms.

```
<input type="text" value="Default text">
```

- `placeholder`
  Provides a hint to users about what they can enter in an input field.

```
<input type="email" placeholder="Enter your email">
```

- `disabled`
  A boolean attribute that disables an element (e.g., a form input).

```
<button disabled>Submit</button>
```

- `readonly`
  Makes input fields non-editable, while still allowing them to be focused and copied.

```
<input type="text" value="Read only" readonly>
```

- `checked`
  A boolean attribute used with checkboxes or radio buttons to indicate a default selected option.

```
<input type="checkbox" checked> I agree to the terms
```

- `name`
  Specifies a name for input elements, allowing them to be identified when the form is submitted.

```
<input type="text" name="username">
```

- `action`
  Defines where the form data should be sent when submitted (usually a URL).

```
<form action="/submit-form" method="post">
```

- `method`
  Specifies how to send form data: either `GET` (for URL parameters) or `POST` (for more secure data submission).

```
<form action="/submit-form" method="post">
```

- `maxlength`
  Limits the number of characters a user can input.

```
<input type="text" maxlength="10">
```

- `data-*`
  Custom data attributes allow you to store extra information in an element, often used in JavaScript.

```
<div data-user-id="123">User Information</div>
```

How Attributes Work Together

Attributes often work in combination. For example, a form input field might include several attributes to specify its behavior:

```
<input type="text" name="username" placeholder="Enter your
username" maxlength="20" required>
```

In this example:

- `type="text"` specifies that this is a text input.
- `name="username"` gives the field a name.
- `placeholder="Enter your username"` provides a hint to the user.
- `maxlength="20"` limits the input to 20 characters.
- `required` ensures that the field must be filled before submitting the form.

Final Thoughts

Attributes are the building blocks of HTML elements, providing important metadata and controlling how elements behave or appear. Understanding these common attributes will allow you to enhance your HTML structure for better design, interactivity, and accessibility.

Chapter 8: Practice Activities

Now that you've learned the basics of HTML, it's time to test your understanding with some hands-on practice. Practice is essential for mastering web development, and the more you code, the more you'll solidify the concepts you've learned.

In this chapter, we will present a series of exercises that focus on key HTML concepts like document structure, text formatting, links, lists, images, and forms. These questions are designed to help you build real-world web pages, and by completing them, you'll gain confidence in applying your HTML knowledge to actual projects.

---

1. Create a Simple Webpage

Question:
Create a basic HTML webpage with the following structure:

- A title in the browser tab that reads "My First Webpage."
- A heading with the text "Welcome to My Webpage."
- A paragraph introducing yourself, including your name and a brief description of what you do.
- Include a horizontal line between the heading and the paragraph.

Hint: Use the `<title>`, `<h1>`, `<p>`, and `<hr>` elements.

---

2. Formatting Text with HTML

Question:
Create a webpage with the following text formatting:

- A heading that says "HTML Text Formatting."
- A paragraph with the following sentence: "HTML allows us to format **bold**, *italic*, and `<u>underlined</u>` text."
- A line break between each formatted word in the paragraph.

Hint: Use `<b>`, `<i>`, `<u>`, and `<br>` elements for formatting text.

3. Creating a List of Hobbies

Question:
Create a webpage with two lists of your hobbies:

1. An unordered list (bulleted) of at least three hobbies you enjoy.
2. An ordered list (numbered) of three goals you have in learning web development.

Hint: Use the `<ul>`, `<ol>`, and `<li>` elements to create lists.

---

4. Adding Links to Your Webpage

Question:
Create a webpage that includes the following:

- A heading with the text "Useful Links."
- A link that directs users to Google with the anchor text "Search on Google."
- A second link that opens in a new tab directing to your favorite website.

Hint: Use the `<a>` element with the `href` attribute. Use the `target="_blank"` attribute to open the link in a new tab.

---

5. Embedding an Image

Question:
Create a webpage that contains:

- A heading with the text "My Favorite Picture."
- An image of your choice (from a URL or a local file).
- A caption below the image with the text "This is my favorite picture."

Hint: Use the `<img>` element with the `src` attribute to add an image, and the `<figcaption>` element to caption it.

---

6. Creating a Contact Form

Question:
Create a basic contact form that includes:

- A text input field labeled "Name."
- An email input field labeled "Email Address."
- A textarea labeled "Message."
- A submit button that says "Send Message."

Hint: Use the `<form>`, `<input>`, `<label>`, `<textarea>`, and `<button>` elements to create the form.

---

7. Adding a Table

Question:
Create a table with the following structure:

- A heading that says "My Schedule."
- The first row contains three column headers: "Day," "Activity," and "Time."
- Add three rows of data where each row represents a day, an activity you do on that day, and the time of the activity.

Hint: Use the `<table>`, `<tr>`, `<th>`, and `<td>` elements to create a table.

---

8. Using HTML Comments

Question:
Create a webpage with the following:

- A heading that says "HTML Comments Practice."
- A paragraph explaining what comments are and how they are used in HTML.
- Somewhere in the HTML code, include a comment that says, "This is a comment that will not be displayed on the webpage."

Hint: Use the `<!-- Comment -->` syntax to insert an HTML comment.

9. Structuring a Webpage with Divs

Question:
Create a webpage with the following sections:

- A header with the text "My Website Header."
- A navigation section with links to "Home," "About," and "Contact."
- A main content section with a paragraph of text.
- A footer with the text "Copyright 2024."

Hint: Use the `<div>` element to structure the different sections of the webpage.

---

10. Embedding a Video

Question:
Create a webpage that embeds a YouTube video of your choice. The video should have a heading that says "Watch This Video" and be centered on the page.

Hint: Use the `<iframe>` element to embed a video from YouTube.

Conclusion

These 10 practice activities are designed to cover a range of essential HTML skills, from text formatting and linking to embedding media and structuring content. By working through these exercises, you will reinforce what you have learned and start applying HTML to real-world scenarios.

As you complete each task, take time to review the output in your browser and ensure that the HTML behaves as expected.

Remember: coding is all about practice. The more you work through exercises like these, the more comfortable you'll become with HTML, and soon you'll be ready to take on more advanced concepts.

Chapter 9: Last Thoughts

As we come to the conclusion of this journey, it's important to step back and reflect on what you've learned about the fundamental building blocks of web development—**HTML,** HTML: The Structure of the Web

HTML (Hypertext Markup Language) is the skeleton of a webpage. It's the foundational language that defines the structure and content. Every element you see on a webpage—headings, paragraphs, images, links—are all defined by HTML. It creates the framework that tells browsers what content is on the page and how it's organized.

By learning HTML, you've acquired the ability to structure content in a logical, hierarchical way. You've learned about different elements, how to create forms, tables, and lists, and how to link to other web pages. These are the basic tools that allow you to create the framework of any website.

Learning HTML is like learning the alphabet—it's the foundation upon which everything else is built. But as with any skill, learning never truly ends. There's always more to explore, experiment with, and refine.

The best way to improve your HTML skills is by applying what you've learned to real-world projects. Start by building small websites, such as personal portfolios, blogs, or simple landing pages. Over time, you can take on more complex projects like creating multi-page websites or experimenting with different content layouts.

Every project will teach you something new, whether it's discovering new HTML elements or finding more efficient ways to organize your code. The more you create, the better you'll understand how HTML works in practice.

Remember, web development is not just about writing code—it's about problem-solving, creativity, and constantly learning. Keep building, keep experimenting, and most importantly, keep enjoying the process.

Thank you for embarking on this journey with me. The web is vast, and there's so much more for you to explore. Now it's time for you to take what you've learned and build something incredible!

Good luck, and happy coding!

About the Author

Roggie (Raj) Clark, is a 9 year SEO professional and owner of the SEO agency; *Bounce Rank.* Prior to joining the SEO industry, Raj was a web developer and school teacher. It was through creating his own websites, and wanting a career change from teaching, that Raj stumbled across the world of SEO.

Since joining the field nearly a decade ago, Raj has worked on a wide range of campaigns, from eCommerce, to B2B, to Healthcare, for enterprise companies and marketing agencies in the United States.

He is regarded as an expert, and guru by his colleagues, and the SEO industry. Raj currently lives in Maryland with his sister and niece.

www.ingramcontent.com/pod-product-compliance
Lightning Source LLC
LaVergne TN
LVHW080001210926
848481LV00012B/3649

* 9 7 9 8 3 3 0 4 5 5 7 9 9 *